PROCRASTINATION PRIORITY

Text **60 Minutes**	The length of our small books is based on the time in the air of a flight between Toronto and Chicago. Start reading as you take off and finish the book by the time you land. Just the right length for the 21st-century reader.
Cartoons **30 Minutes**	You can also gain a complete overview of the ideas in this book by looking at the cartoons and reading the captions. We find the cartoons have made our Strategic Coach concepts accessible to readers as young as eight years old.
Audio **120 Minutes**	The audio recording that accompanies this book is not just a recitation of the printed words but an in-depth commentary that expands each chapter's mindset into new dimensions. Download the audio at **strategiccoach.com/go/procrastination**.
Video **60 Minutes**	Our video synopsis of Procrastination Priority deepens your understanding of all eight mindsets. If you combine text, cartoons, audio, and video, your understanding of the ideas will be 10x greater than you would gain from reading only. Watch the videos at **strategiccoach.com/go/procrastination**.
Scorecard **10 Minutes**	Fold out the back cover of this book to score your Procrastination Priority mindset. First, score yourself on where you are now, and then fill in where you want to be a year from now. Download additional copies at **strategiccoach.com/go/procrastination**.
ebook **1 Minute**	After absorbing the fundamental ideas of the Procrastination Priority concept, you can quickly and easily share them by sending the ebook version to as many other individuals as you desire. Direct them to **strategiccoach.com/go/procrastination**.

Thanks to the Creative Team:

Kerri Morrison

Adam Morrison

Hamish MacDonald

Shannon Waller

Jennifer Bhatthal

Victor Lam

Suzanne Noga

Margaux Yiu

Christine Nishino

Willard Bond

Procrastination Priority

This little book will enable you to perform a mind-set miracle in the 60 minutes it takes to read it. This remarkable shift will come from seeing every kind of procrastination in your life—past, present, and future—as a uniquely transformative growth opportunity. Instead of feeling embarrassed, guilty, paralyzed, or isolated by procrastination, you'll now realize that something extraordinary is possible.

Not only is procrastination not a negative part of your life, it's the guaranteed trigger for your most creative and productive achievements. You'll discover from this very fast read that procrastination can permanently become your best way each night to know with confident certainty what your three most important priorities for achievement will be for tomorrow—for the rest of your life.

Strategic Coach®, The Strategic Coach® Program, The Self-Managing Company®, The 4 C's Formula®, The Self-Multiplying Company™, Unique Ability® Team, The Strategic Coach® Signature Program, and The 10x Ambition Program™ are trademarks of The Strategic Coach Inc.

Cartoons by Hamish MacDonald.

Printed in Toronto, Canada. The Strategic Coach Inc., 33 Fraser Avenue, Suite 201, Toronto, Ontario, M6K 3J9.

This publication is meant to strengthen your common sense, not to substitute for it. It is also not a substitute for the advice of your doctor, lawyer, accountant, or any of your advisors, personal or professional.

If you would like further information about The Strategic Coach® Program or other Strategic Coach® services and products, please telephone 416.531.7399 or 1.800.387.3206.

Library and Archives Canada Cataloguing in Publication

Sullivan, Dan, 1944-, author
    Procrastination priority / Dan Sullivan.

ISBN 978-1-897239-50-6 (softcover)

    1. Procrastination. 2. Motivation (Psychology). 3. Goal (Psychology). I. Title.

BF637.P76 S85 2017   155.2'32   C2017-902859-6

Contents

Introduction
I'm Dan, And I'm A Procrastinator
You tell yourself the truth that throughout your life, you've frequently found yourself "stuck" in your thinking, decision-making, and actions.

When I started talking about procrastination in my workshops, something funny happened. I discovered that most of the entrepreneurs in my workshop groups assumed that I never procrastinate. They were shocked to think that I would ever fall into such a bad habit as procrastination.

But here's the truth: Everyone procrastinates. And, what's more, it's not such a bad habit after all.

So right off the bat, I'm going to admit that I'm a procrastinator. And I hope you'll now feel comfortable to admit that you procrastinate as well.

Procrastination lived rent-free in my brain for years, but now I've put it to work and am reaping the benefits of all it has to offer.

Liberating new lifetime capability.
Most people experience procrastination as something negative. They don't want to talk about it because they feel guilty about doing it and think others would think less of them if they found out. They look around and get the impression that everyone else has it all together, and they feel isolated and guilty about putting off important tasks and goals and feeling stuck.

But procrastination is a normal human experience—and it's okay to talk about it.

In working with entrepreneurs, I've seen that telling the truth about procrastination and being able to talk about it is a breakthrough in and of itself.

This breakthrough is the first step in allowing you to understand that you can respond to procrastination in a way that's really quite extraordinarily creative. It fundamentally changes how you look at yourself and how you look at challenges in your life that may be overwhelming at first or are bigger than your present capability. It helps to acknowledge that feeling stuck and trapped is a normal part of growing and expanding.

People compare themselves to others without realizing that there's a "front stage" and "backstage" to life. If you're in the modern workplace, there's enormous emphasis on looking good and appearing to have your act together.

We feel guilty about our procrastination when we compare our backstage to other people's front stage and worry that others will lose confidence in us if we admit that we're procrastinating about things. There's also an internal sense of guilt that we've been wasting time and energy in procrastinating and that that time and energy will be lost forever.

But simply telling the truth about procrastination is a liberating capability you can acquire and develop that will free your thinking from decades of guilt associated with perceived wasted time and energy.

"Lost" time returned to you.
A lot of people feel under the gun to get as much done as

they can in the shortest amount of time, feeling pressure from deadlines and expectations. There's a negative judgment about procrastination because it's seen as a time when you weren't being efficient or productive, moving ahead, getting things done, or keeping up with others. You have the sense that you've lost time when you've procrastinated. And in a world of efficiency, losing time is a sin.

But with a shift in your perspective, you'll see that none of that time was meaningless. All the time you felt was lost through procrastination will suddenly become valuable and useful to you.

You'll recognize that the time when you felt trapped and stuck was actually very creative time, and you couldn't have come up with the solutions you later did unless you'd been willing to give yourself that time. In retrospect, the time always looks wasted because the solution now seems obvious. But it wasn't obvious. You needed the time to create the solution. So, in fact, there was no time lost.

"Wasted" energy returned to you.
Something I've experienced with procrastination is that there's a lot of energy that gets used, but it's negative energy and it seems to be for no purpose.

You feel that if only you could have captured that energy and focused it on something productive, it would be worthwhile. But this is not taking into account that, in life, we're in a constant discovery process.

When we're dealing with things in our lives that really matter, we're always going from one level of understanding to a higher level of understanding, and that jump takes time and energy. This is how learning and growth take place. It's not wasted.

Your whole future transforms right now.
Mindset has to be the start of any change. Unlike shifts in knowledge, skills, or habits, a shift in mindset can take place in an instant.

My aim is that, during the course of reading this small book, you'll feel transformed by the very idea that your procrastination throughout your lifetime has not been a bad thing but an extraordinary hidden resource that will multiply starting today.

It can be deeply destructive to people's confidence to look at procrastination as wasted time and energy. To do this is to continually depreciate and devalue your past experience precisely because of the procrastination that took place while you were gaining that experience.

A shift occurs when you take on the mindset that procrastination is actually extremely useful.

Today's procrastination sets up tomorrow.
This shift will also impact the way you see yourself. You'll realize that anytime you're procrastinating, you're doing so for a good reason, and you'll learn to determine what that reason is.

But perhaps the most significant insight you'll gain is that the situations in which you feel most stuck and trapped right now are actually your surest and most dependable priorities for making decisions and taking action tomorrow.

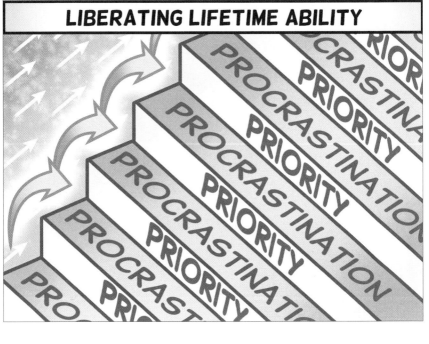

Chapter 1
Everybody Procrastinates

You happily admit that you're a procrastinator because so is everybody else.

The vast majority of people procrastinate in certain kinds of situations, and entrepreneurs are no exception.

Entrepreneurs tell me that they dread the times they're procrastinating and that the worst experiences from their pasts were when they were stuck and felt paralyzed, unable to move forward, especially when other people were depending on them for something and they weren't delivering. It's a painful experience.

But what is procrastination? I've found that when it comes to procrastinating, "should" tends to be the operative word. You either *shouldn't* be doing something but you're still doing it, or you *should* do something but you aren't doing it. The word "should" involves second-guessing yourself, being your own critic, and being negatively judged by yourself or by other people.

Procrastination is something that entrepreneurs feel both guilty about and isolated about in their work life, but it's important for everyone to acknowledge that procrastinating is a universal experience.

100 billion people have done it.

Procrastinating is as natural as breathing. Every human who has ever lived has procrastinated. It's just a part of how the human brain works. So it seems absurd for it to be a source of guilt or cause feelings of isolation. But because it's so often a source of guilt, people hide it. And it's the hiding of it that damages one's confidence and one's ability to move forward.

My solution? Bring it out in the open. Once you realize that everybody has felt paralyzed in their thinking and actions by something at some point, you can happily admit that you do it too, and it can become a normal topic of discussion with others and free you from feelings of guilt.

This shift in how you think about procrastination can be the start of one of the most transformative experiences of your life: By changing your mindset, you can transform every pro-crastination you have experienced in your life into a positive and creative capability.

Everybody's procrastinating about something.

When a new situation triggers a sense of paralysis, it's okay to be temporarily paralyzed by it, but the problem is that it tends to linger. And the longer it lingers, the more likely you are to feel guilty about procrastinating and frustrated by a sense of feeling stuck.

But knowing you're not alone in this can make all the differ-ence. You can take it for granted that everyone you know is a procrastinator and that each of them is trying to hide it. It's almost like a universal conspiracy of humanity against itself. You've got all these people walking around with a secret, preventing themselves from moving forward, feeling guilty and feeling judged—including harshly judged by them-selves—and it's doing no good.

When this happens, people tend to isolate themselves from others. And when people get isolated, they start making up things that aren't true. The fantasies or hallucinations they create actually make the situation worse, leading to a down-ward spiral.

It all comes from the feeling that there's something they need to hide from others because they believe if other people knew it, they'd be rejected and discounted. People who don't know that everybody else is also procrastinating don't feel that they can discuss it in an open way.

It's time to do something different.

But if you can have a general discussion about procrastination as a natural process, you won't just get rid of the negative, you'll release an extraordinary amount of cooperative energy.

Indeed, simply admitting that you're a procrastinator enables you to think and act in a new, different, and better way.

The next step is to look at *why* people procrastinate. Generally speaking, children aren't self-judgmental like adults are. This is because they live mostly in the present. The moment you start developing a future time sense and a past time sense, you begin to make judgments about whether you're performing properly and moving along properly, because you're making comparisons to other people. At a certain stage of mental development, you start operating in three time senses: past, present, and future. It's at that point that procrastination comes into play.

New way of looking at everything.

At the moment you're in a position where striving for something in the future becomes a conscious act, procrastination sets in. If you hear "should" enough times from outside sources, it's likely that you'll internalize it to some degree, and both self-judgment and this internalization of critical judgment contribute an enormous amount to why people procrastinate, how they procrastinate, and how long they're trapped in the procrastination.

But judgment doesn't do you any good. There's a huge difference between judging your progress, which is demo-tivating, and measuring your progress, which is motivating. Judgment just produces the desire not to be judged. It's a defensive reaction.

It could be your greatest new ability.

Measurement, on the other hand, produces a motivation to exceed your previous measurements. It's an expansive reaction. Through measurement, you can draw lessons from the difference between what you did yesterday, what you're doing today, and what you can do tomorrow.

If we focus on judging ourselves for procrastinating, we lose any confidence or momentum we had. Why don't we release all the negative energy associated with procrasti-nation and turn it into a positive? It's time to do something different.

Simply looking differently at something that's always stopped you can actually be a new way to always get you moving.

In the following chapters, we'll look at a way to transform your current thinking about procrastination and instead use procrastination as a tool for future growth.

Chapter 2
Always For Good Reasons
You fully accept that there's always a perfectly intelligent reason why you're procrastinating.

One of the things that prompts people to procrastinate and to hide their procrastination is the feeling that they're being cowardly, that it's a character flaw, and that they're cutting themselves off from the stream of great achievers who get results. This is because they believe there's no good reason why they're procrastinating.

Looking deeper for the cause.
But it's a mistake to think this way. In fact, it's likely there's a very good reason for your procrastination—even an intelligent one.

The intelligent reason is that you've visualized something for yourself in the future that your present level of capability and confidence can't pull off. You're simply making an accurate assessment of the gap between where you are now and where you want to be.

You're recognizing that based on what you're capable of now, both practically and emotionally, you can't pull off the goal. This is a perfectly intelligent reason to pause and think it through.

Opportunity to be smarter.
Procrastination in any situation always reveals some important knowledge or capability that's missing, and this is why progress has stopped. The moment you feel yourself procrastinating, ask yourself the question, "Why am I procrastinating here?"

Don't put a negative spin on it; simply observe that you've now gone into a mental state called procrastination and know that the proper response to that is to ask why.

In fact, you're only procrastinating to the point that you ask yourself why. Once you ask why, you start to break the power of procrastination.

Now, you're into the transformative mode because you can write down the reasons you're procrastinating. As long as you're willing to accept the reasons as being intelligent, and that it makes total sense why you would be procrastinating in this situation, you're entirely transforming this experience.

The feeling of procrastination is very natural, and if it immediately triggers you to find out the deeper reason, then this is an extraordinarily creative and positive ability.

Procrastination is the bell that goes off, suddenly alerting you to the fact that you've just visualized something that's bigger and better than your existing levels of capability and confidence. It lets you know that you need to approach the situation differently and that you've been challenged to get smarter with regard to it.

Every time you have a feeling of procrastination, you're going to get the chance to understand yourself better.

You're going to understand more deeply and more expansively that in this type of situation, it's appropriate to think things through. It's not appropriate to take action right now.

The procrastination is just an alert that you've reached the edge of your own capabilities and your own level of confidence. Perhaps someone else's capability and confidence need to be brought in.

Preparation for something new.

A lot of people cut themselves off from having big goals because it results in that negative feeling of procrastination. But not having goals doesn't help them. They're misinterpreting what the feeling of procrastination actually means: It's a natural response to envisioning a bigger future, which immediately throws a spotlight on your present deficiencies related to the bigger result and bigger performance needed to reach it.

Procrastinating might feel like you're failing, but you're just in the early stages of growing to the next level. The procrastination is a dial on the wall telling you this is a growth period right now, and you have to jump to a higher level.

There's something new you need to learn and master. It also means that you're probably going to increase your teamwork with people who have capabilities that are better suited to the goal ahead.

Procrastination is always a message that your brain is sending to you that you've just visualized something that's going to require you to play a new game. You're being asked to have a bigger picture of your future than what was true before.

The moment you change the picture in your mind of what your future could be, it's going to change how you use your existing capabilities and your present level of confidence, and it's going to call for you to raise your levels of both.

You at your most unique.
The obstacle of procrastination you experience reveals that you're holding back until you can see how to move forward in a uniquely creative way.

The interaction, or the tension, between your visualizing a bigger and better future and experiencing procrastination places you right at the heart of your uniqueness. Nobody else has that vision, and nobody else has that particular reason for procrastinating. In fact, you might be procrastinating on doing something the conventional way so that you can, instead, figure out your own creative approach.

Remarkable shift in thinking.
Every procrastination in your life—past, present, and future—is an opportunity for a shift in thinking. The shift might be big or small. Your visualizing the future is unpredictable, what stops you about that vision is unpredictable, and how you transform it is unpredictable.

By examining why you're procrastinating, you can find a rich area for intellectual and creative transformation in what's essentially a dead zone of human activity. It's very rich in possibilities once you get rid of the negativity.

When people suddenly realize that an activity they've felt guilty about all their lives is actually the key to their bigger and better future, that's when the transformation happens.

Chapter 3
Caused By Your Ambition
You realize that procrastination always comes from wanting something bigger and better.

The price of being visionary is that it upsets your present.

The moment you see something you want but don't have, you've just disrupted your general feeling of contentment with what you've got, and this mental leap ahead immediately sets you up for procrastination.

The price of seeing the future.
Procrastination comes from wanting something bigger and better than you have right now. If you're someone who simply maintains the status quo, you're less likely to procrastinate because ambition won't require you to do something different. Being ambitious and being a procrastinator are directly linked to each other. Both are part of the same growth process that keeps making you more capable and confident.

Ambition isn't always seen as a negative in the way that procrastination is, but it's stated as a criticism as often as it's intended as praise or admiration. There's the sense that there's something unmanageable and uncontrollable about people giving free rein to their ambition, and one of the reasons we haven't yet come to grips with procrastination being okay or even a positive thing is that there generally wasn't admiration for individual ambition, especially when it was being used to take control of an existing system.

Indeed, another reason procrastination is seen as negative is because even the greater ambition that triggered the procrastination was something a lot of people have been told to hide. Many successful entrepreneurs still experience a hesitancy with their family, friends, and community to express their ambition. They can't be unabashedly ambitious except with other like-minded entrepreneurs.

On the other hand, strong ambition is generally accepted by others if you're creating something outside of an existing system and if what you're creating is something brand new that will bring a new kind of value.

Immediately, you're deficient.

All goals start in your imagination, which doesn't distinguish between reality and fiction. You can see a future reality and immediately intellectually engage with it and emotionally commit yourself to it before you've even thought it through.

Once you come back to your present, though, you realize that your current levels of capability and confidence won't be sufficient to achieve that jump to higher performance, achievement, and results. So, the bigger vision ahead makes you feel deficient right now.

There's also a tension in very talented people that comes from there being a huge gulf between how other people are seeing them and how they see themselves. They feel like phonies because the things they hear people saying about them have no relationship with how they think about the experiences they're going through.

And the clock is ticking.

We visualize in a "timeless zone." There's no clock ticking as you experience your bigger future vision, but the moment you're back in the present, you're back in "real time," and time becomes a factor.

First of all, virtually all of the time ahead of you is already spoken for, so a disruption to your time management comes in. There's an immediate sense of a scarcity of time for completing this larger endeavor. Not only that, but you haven't yet put a date to when this goal should happen, but you feel the sooner you get to this new state, the better. So you immediately feel that you're running out of time.

Existing capabilities won't do.
Feeling trapped between the highly desirable future and the suddenly deficient present brings on paralysis.

People say, "I feel stuck," and I believe it's more than just a metaphor or a mental state. I think they feel physically stuck. When you see a goal, you see the *how* and the *what* and the *when*, but you don't see the *why*, and the reason you get stuck is you're lacking the *why*.

You can't shift your mindset until you approach your procrastination with the question of why this is happening. You know that existing capabilities won't do to reach the goal, because existing capabilities are based on a *why* from the past.

Once you see the new vision, the previous *why*—which was perfectly good for you to be able to do what you're doing today—is no longer sufficient.

You have to establish a new *why*, and you probably won't change from doing what works right now unless the *why* is good enough to motivate that change.

No alternative except growth.

The reason a lot of people don't like growing is that, in its early stages, it's not a positive experience. It's uncomfortable because you're filled with adrenaline that's pushing you forward, but you're lacking the capability that would ideally go along with it.

All the adrenaline is doing is getting you ready for the job. If you're going to be fully human and feel yourself being more fully human every year, there's going to be a steady diet of this, and it's going to last for the rest of your life.

The paralyzing experience of procrastination points to the only way forward: taking your existing capability and confidence to a higher level in order to be able to achieve the bigger and better goal. Once you've entertained a vision that you've intellectually and emotionally engaged with, and you've committed to it to the point where it's disrupting your sense of your present level of capability, the only good option is to grow into that vision. Recognizing this can help shake off the paralysis.

Doing this over and over makes you better at it. You feel the fear and the paralysis, and you say to yourself, "I'm just scared of something bigger, so let's get going on it. I'm going to go through the fear now, or I'm going to go through the fear tomorrow, or I'm going to go through the fear a month from now. But I have to go through the fear. It's natural that I should be uncomfortable. It's natural that I should feel anxious because this is what growth feels like."

Changing your mindset and inner narrative in this way has the remarkable ability to move you forward toward your goals.

Chapter 4
Challenged To Grow
You understand that all challenges to personally grow start with upfront fear and discomfort.

Rather than simply being an obstacle to progress, your pro-crastinations can be the key to your growth—if you're willing to push through feelings of fear and uncertainty brought on by your bigger future goals.

Anxiety is the advantage.
The anxiety you feel when you're procrastinating is a nec-essary experience because you can use the discomfort to identify where exactly you need to grow new capability in order to achieve your goal.

Moreover, if the energy from a new goal first comes in the form of negativity, you'll be more energized to make a shift. You have to start with the negative energy in order to get to the positive energy because otherwise you wouldn't have the motivation.

If it were a strictly pleasant experience that came from the future vision, it wouldn't necessarily prompt you to do any-thing. You might just coast along. The experience of being disrupted and thrown off balance is crucial to the personal change you have to go through. And when you experience the shift from negative to positive, you can feel it in your mind, in your body, and in your energy.

First, intellectual commitment.
When you first decide on a goal, your brain looks for the simplest, easiest solutions. You want to solve 20 problems without having to do 20 things. You check to see how some-thing can work with what you're already doing. You want

consistency or a multiplication of what you already have. You want the next level that maximizes the use of the level you're already on.

The more you can intellectually engage with how and when something is going to happen, the better. This is how you commit to achieving measurable progress toward a bigger and better goal and specify a deadline for your progress.

Having engaged intellectually, you're now committed emotionally to going through the process of change and improvement that the intellectual engagement has indicated.

But once you've done the intellectual engagement and com- mitment, you can't fool around. The more you allow yourself to be paralyzed by anxiety, the worse the anxiety will get.

Anxiety is useful as long as it doesn't last for too long. It's a fuel that has to be immediately used for decision-making, communication, and action.

Then, courageous movement forward.
When you're paralyzed by procrastination, you're in what I call "The No Zone." You're stuck, and you don't even have access to your existing level of confidence and capabilities. You're also completely unable to access capabilities and resources that lie in others. You're not connected with any- thing that can improve your situation.

Only taking action can alleviate the anxiety, and if you don't take action, the tension will do you in. It's better to be in a state of forward fear than it is to be paralyzed because you can do something with the forward motion and with the fear.

As soon as you move, you escape your procrastination. If you ask entrepreneurs about the most memorable part of their careers, they'll tell you it was when they were in a state of fear moving toward something bigger and better.

When you're in a moving state of fear and discomfort, you can access your existing level of capability and confidence, and the forward motion will create new capability. You can't learn anything when you're paralyzed. It's when you're actually testing, failing, and learning that the capability develops. This is "The Grow Zone."

The discomfort of stretching.

Being courageous before you're more capable is uncomfortable because it involves stretching into a bigger version of yourself. The best possible way to improve is to be willing to put yourself in this state of discomfort, uncertainty, and anxiety, and use it to spur yourself into action.

Fear clarifies and simplifies everything. When you're in a state of fear, you don't have the luxury of having secondary thoughts. You're 100 percent in the main activity, and there's no room for distractions. You have to follow through because you don't want this uncomfortable state to last forever.

Though courage is necessary, it doesn't mean that you want it to be a long-term experience. The way to cut it short is to commit yourself 100 percent right off the bat to going through it. Any falling off from 100 percent commitment extends the length of time you're going to have to spend in the courage stage. If you're only half scared, that period of courage is going to be four times as long.

Best possible way to improve.

I know a lot of people who are unhappy as they get older because they've never really come to grips with the challenge of growth. They try to avoid it and to surround themselves with other people who don't challenge themselves to grow. They become increasingly miserable from the lack of growth. Getting older without growing is a terrible experience.

Transforming your understanding of procrastination and making use of it to grow is the way to confidently improve every part of your life in a way that's always exciting and satisfying.

Keep in mind that identifying that you're procrastinating about something doesn't mean that you instantly have to take action on it. It may not be a high enough priority. You might be able to come up with ten procrastinations and only have time for three, so the rest will have to take a ticket and wait in line.

That said, having identified something as a top-priority procrastination takes you out of the negative zone as long as you get to it in a timely fashion or eliminate it as a goal altogether, replacing the wish with a solution that doesn't require you to endlessly wish for it.

Viewing your procrastinations in this way, you can now see that they're actually something to get excited about. Going forward, you'll recognize that your procrastination is an indication that there's an area in which you need to grow. Each procrastination represents an opportunity for change and progress.

Chapter 5
Start With The Truth

You always tell the truth about each procrastination in order to create greater commitment and courage.

Being a procrastinator shouldn't make you feel invalidated. Procrastination is a completely natural thing that people do. All of the problems associated with procrastination have to do with people not telling the truth—which is that they procrastinate.

It's important to start recognizing that procrastination is an indicator that you need to go deeper with your thinking about what you're procrastinating on and that you're dealing with new circumstances that require reevaluation. In other words, procrastination is a trigger for an entirely new way of thinking about things.

Where all progress starts.

All the feelings of guilt, isolation, pressure, and anxiety you experience when you're procrastinating will disappear the moment you simply tell the truth about why you're not moving forward and discover the essential answer as to why you're procrastinating.

The reason usually falls into one or more of the following categories: 1. You've become aware of the fact that you need a higher confidence level to achieve the result. 2. You need more capability than you presently have. 3. You don't have enough time because your future time, leading up to the goal, is already accounted for by your present activities. 4. You're confronted with the fact that the capabilities and time required to get things done means teamwork with others, and you have a deficiency of teamwork right now.

Regardless of the reason, when you tell the truth about a procrastination, you automatically trigger new commitment and courage in yourself to move forward and become more capable and confident. Within each of your procrastinations lies a new truth. If you tell the truth that you're procrastinating and then look deeper into the procrastination, something new about what you're thinking and what's possible will be revealed.

All thinking integrated again.

When you go through periods of procrastination, it's best to experience the paralysis and recognize it for what it is without self-judging. Taking the judgment out of the equation will free you to see the reality more clearly.

If you very quickly move on to the next step and tell yourself why you got stopped, all of a sudden, a lot of energy will return to you, your confidence will start to come back, and you'll become clear again on how to move forward. Whereas you were kind of scattered before, everything will now come back in a unified form.

When you're procrastinating, you get cut off from anything in the future that's really motivating you, so you don't have the value of your future. You also get cut off from things that you already know how to do. You're cut off from access to your previous capability and confidence.

The moment you commit again and set a goal, all of your previous capabilities, experience, and lessons become available to you again. You suddenly feel that you're completely unified and simple in thinking about your next course of action and the progress you're going to make.

Complexity becomes simple.

The reason you set a goal is because you want a result that's bigger and better in the future. But what immediately happens is that you realize you currently don't have the capability, confidence, or time to pull it off. These have suddenly become very complex elements, and you can feel overwhelmed by the complexity you see when you consider the situation. This is the paralyzing factor.

The moment you tell the truth and become committed, your commitment unifies everything. It provides a sharp focus because there's a result you're going to achieve, and that result is measurable. All of your energies become focused, and everything becomes simple and straightforward.

The only way that complexity gets solved is by making a commitment that you're going to achieve something. You can't find simplicity just by analyzing complexity. That will just lead to more complexity.

There has to be action, there has to be commitment, and there has to be courage. These are the elements that simplify complexity.

Complication becomes clear.

While complexity involves more factors than you expected, complication also involves conflict. In other words, aspects of your new goal will likely conflict with things you already have going on. Some of your new ideas might conflict with some of your old ideas, and your new goal might call for some kind of action that conflicts with some of your old habits.

You can be left feeling conflicted about what to concentrate on in order to move forward. But telling the truth about why you're procrastinating and in what way you're procrastinating will immediately clarify exactly where you should now focus your best efforts and energy.

Only you know the solution.

You might have been looking at external factors for the reasons why you couldn't move forward, but nobody else can come up with those reasons because nobody else understands what's going on in your procrastination.

You're always procrastinating for unique reasons, and the uniqueness comes from you. All of the reasons and all of the solutions you need lie in your uniquely transforming your procrastination.

The only possible solution to everything you experience during procrastination comes from your telling the truth— that you're procrastinating—and telling the truth as to why you're procrastinating.

Once you do this, you can recognize what changes you need to make and then focus on achieving a committed, bigger result. Add in the willingness to go through a courageous period in order to actually do it.

Then, all of a sudden, you're going through it. You're out of the procrastination, and you're on to the new thing that you've anticipated. You're in motion, you've got energy, and you're starting to feel the new capability and higher confidence.

Chapter 6
Turn Weakness Into Great Strength
You love that what previously embarrassed you is now your biggest motivator.

When people look back on things they found to be great challenges, huge obstacles, or very stressful situations, the one common feature in all of those experiences tends to be that they spent a significant amount of time in that situation procrastinating.

A great deal of the negativity that people remember when they look back on those situations doesn't come from them having gone up against something that was challenging. A challenge in and of itself, if we've got ourselves together, isn't negative. It might be scary, but it's not negative to be faced with something that forces us to grow.

Rather, the real negative part of almost any challenging experience we've had was the procrastination part that we feel guilty about.

The other part of the experience might have been scary or perhaps physically trying, but when you're committed and have courage, you don't necessarily experience those things as negative. Rather, you likely experience them as positive and feel a sense of pride.

It may be the case that many of people's negative memories are defined by the procrastination they went through during their past experiences.

Because of the judgment that comes with procrastination, you might not want to remember those parts of the negative experiences, and so the periods of procrastination are the only parts of the experiences you don't learn from.

But with this new way of looking at procrastination, this thing that previously embarrassed you can now be your biggest motivator. Once you remove the judgment, you can see these huge pools of opportunity for learning in your past. You now know that your periods of procrastination, which you had considered as being among the worst experiences of your past, were actually entirely useful attempts to create greater capability and confidence.

Loneliest part of people's lives.

In the past, when you've procrastinated, you've isolated yourself from other people because you didn't want them to know that you were procrastinating, that you felt incapable, and that you weren't confident. You felt disconnected and utterly lonely. You felt there wasn't anyone else in the world who understood what you were going through. And there was no one else who actually understood what it was that you were procrastinating about, because it was unique to you.

But while you're the only one who can solve your unique procrastination, you never have to have that disconnected and lonely feeling again.

You can always tell the truth about what you're going through. At no moment are you cut off from the ability to tell the truth. I've found that regardless of what I might be procrastinating about, there's a peaceful feeling that comes when I recognize what's happening and have the courage to tell the truth about it.

When we're not hiding what's going on, there's no reason why we should cut ourselves off from others and not receive help that could be available to us.

Being your own worst critic.

A common response to procrastination is to beat yourself up, to be self-judgmental and negative. But by not being willing to tell the truth about this or to understand the dynamics that actually occur when you're procrastinating, you're cutting yourself off from self-knowledge. Instead, recognize that all of the elements of your procrastination — including what you're procrastinating about, where you're doing the procrastinating, and in what way you're procrasti- nating — are all superb indicators of your uniqueness.

Treat yourself as special, and know that by transforming each of your procrastinations as soon as they come up, you'll never again be your own worst critic. Instead, you'll more and more become your own best friend and ally.

Breaking out of self-prison.

On all of those occasions when you were seemingly wasting time procrastinating, it was really part of your growth, part of a learning process. Those times that you thought were worthless actually had great value, and you now know that you never have to go through that difficult and negative experience again.

Feeling guilty and isolated because of procrastination is like being in a prison of your own making. But now you're released from that prison, and recognizing that procrastina- tion is okay gives you a retroactive blanket pardon.

Ability to make up for lost time.

A lot of your mental energy gets tied up with feelings of guilt over past procrastinations. But when you acknowledge that there were good reasons behind them, you're released from the negative feelings toward them in the present, freeing up your mental energy for more creative things.

Moreover, when you take away the judgment from your past experiences of procrastination, you can see that the time you spent procrastinating wasn't, in fact, time wasted. There's actually growth and learning during periods of pro- crastination. But because you've assigned a generally bad judgment to the whole experience, you can't appreciate that growth and learning.

As a result of each of your procrastinations, your abilities jumped to the next level and you became wiser. All of that time you thought you'd wasted in procrastination can now return to you in the form of extraordinary ambition.

All trapped energy is released.

There is a strong correlation between experiencing procras- tination and having big goals. Since procrastination occurs when we envision something that's bigger and better than what we already have, some people try to avoid having big goals in order to avoid the negative feelings about them- selves that come as a result of procrastinating.

Once you understand that every period of procrastination that's happened in your life was actually a positive thing, all of that energy from each of those experiences will be released for the purpose of achieving extraordinarily bigger and better future results.

Chapter 7
Each Day's Best Progress
You're excited that your biggest obstacles today can always create your best progress tomorrow.

You could go the rest of your life without doing the regular kind of goal-setting you're used to if you substitute it with a new daily practice: Each night, identify the three biggest things you're procrastinating on. These become your three priorities for tomorrow.

This is because inside every procrastination is a goal.

By making it a daily activity to look at your procrastinations and use them to determine what your priorities are for the next day, you're taking an entirely different approach to both goal-setting and the way you view procrastination.

With this new perspective on procrastination, you start by identifying what you're procrastinating on, and that becomes your new goal. In this way, your biggest obstacles today can create your best progress tomorrow.

If I've done my job up until now, not only should you no longer feel negatively toward procrastination or guilty about it, but you should appreciate that it can be one of your greatest fundamental thinking tools.

Best of all, this thinking tool is built in. There's nothing you have to develop. You've been developing your procrastination skills all your life.

The best confidence of all.
Because of the difficulty and negativity we encounter while we're procrastinating, breaking out of procrastination results

in the finest feeling of confidence we get. When we gain the new capability and feel confident as a result of it, we truly appreciate that newfound confidence because of the sharp contrast between this feeling and what we were experiencing while procrastinating.

Your understanding of how to transform every procrastination means that from now on, you'll always be gaining this kind of confidence simply by visualizing a bigger and better future.

Obstacles no longer negative.
Procrastination feels like not growing, and we can recognize this because we know what growth feels like. Suddenly not experiencing a sense of growth can be uncomfortable, even painful.

But rather than being a period of not growing, procrastination is the necessary result of encountering obstacles that will show you how and where to grow next.

Procrastination is triggered because you've set a big goal and suddenly sense an obstacle in your way. You're meeting this resistance because your vision of a much bigger and better future is also highlighting where you need to increase your capability and confidence.

The obstacles you encounter are there for you to become something more than you currently are. They're there for you to grow in your confidence, thinking abilities, decision-making abilities, and visualization-building.

You only get to create a bigger future by transforming the

obstacles you experience in the present. Every one of the obstacles you run into, all of those things that seem to stand in opposition to your goals, are actually the raw material for you to use in achieving them.

Unlimited raw material.
Where humanity's at its best is in flipping negatives into positives. This takes real uniqueness and creativity, and it's what transforms breakdowns into breakthroughs.

We imagine the future, and in doing so, we present our-selves with obstacles. The obstacles we present ourselves with are the very things we have to deal with in order to arrive at what we envision.

More than most people, entrepreneurs are able to turn this into a way of life, a self-generating way of making a living in the marketplace.

Luxuriate in the fact that you have this ability to continually supply unlimited raw material for your personal growth. All it involves is engaging with the obstacles that tempt you to procrastinate as a result of seeing something bigger and better in the future, and then being very clear that you're involved in this process and that there's no other process more central to who you are and what makes you truly unique. It's what makes you constantly grow in your under-standing and capabilities in the world.

Increasingly useful to everyone else.
The capability you develop of transforming your present pro-crastinations into greater capability and confidence automati-cally makes you into a great teacher and coach who can help others to be transformers of their own procrastination.

Often when great trainers, coaches, or leaders work with people, they help coach them through their procrastinations, but they never put a positive spin on the activity of procrastination. They have the attitude of, "Let's get through this as fast as we can." They don't validate the activity of procrastination, and so people are left feeling dependent on the coach, like the solution came from outside of themselves.

But you don't require any outside agency to move you forward. You have your own internal agency to move yourself forward under any circumstances at any time. It's an especially great ability for entrepreneurs to have, because you've committed your life to being self-generating.

Getting stronger every day.

Procrastination is an area that's hidden in most people, and there's a lack of understanding and appreciation of what's going on there. But it's important to recognize that the process of procrastination is a really useful internal capability and that it can become the basis for an extraordinary breakout ability—an extraordinary way of making personal progress that can become a daily habit.

In understanding this, you gain the greatest confidence about your individual future that anyone can have: You will always have a continually growing ability to transform what you'd previously seen as your worst weakness into your greatest strength.

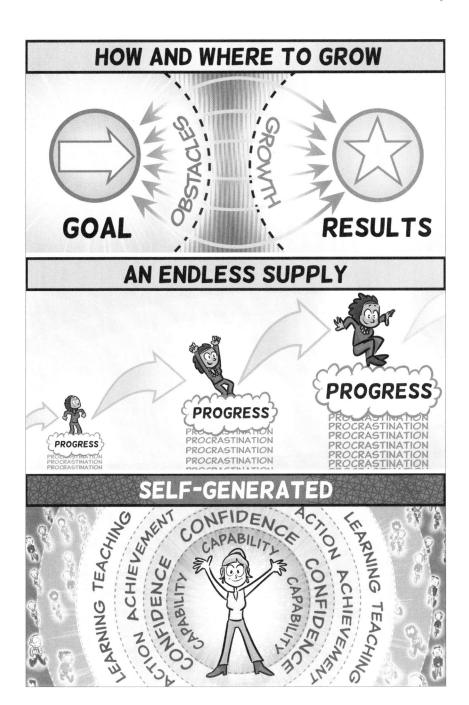

Chapter 8
Procrastination Becomes Priority
You use three procrastinations each evening to achieve three big improvements the next day.

The supply of procrastinations you'll have to transform over your life and career is endless. It's the nature of our minds to see possibilities and improvements, and this sets up our notion of deficiencies, which leads us to procrastinate on our goals.

This occurs in a continuous loop, and you can either wait for it to stop because you've gotten so clogged up with procrastinations that your mind just shuts off—or you can use the procrastinations to your benefit.

As I mentioned in the previous chapter, the best process to make use of your procrastinations is by choosing three of them to focus on at a time. Every evening, select three things that you're procrastinating on, and the next day, turn those three procrastinations into three big achievements.

In reading and listening to this book, and adopting the mindsets and processes I've discussed, you'll be taking the experience that's probably continually been the source of your greatest negativity and stress and transforming it not only into something positive and promising, but into your single most important daily focus and activity.

Everything you'll ever need.
In your growing ability to visualize an always bigger and better future, and then to always tell the truth and transform your emerging procrastinations, you have everything you need to continually become more capable and confident.

It's a closed-loop cycle that's always going. With every pro-crastination, you pull in the raw material that identifies some sort of deficiency. It's a momentary obstacle you transform into decisions, communications, actions, and established deadlines. You commit yourself to a goal, which requires courage, and you acquire a new capability and new con-fidence from pursuing the goal. This is a complete growth cycle, and you'll never run out of material for it.

Minding your procrastination.

You now have a single most important focus: using your creative mind to envision the best possible day tomorrow, and to have every one of your days be more successful and satisfying than the last. All you have to do is identify where and why you're procrastinating.

If you write down five or six of your current procrastinations, you'll immediately know which are the three most important ones, because your mind has already given a great deal of thought to this. In this permanent daily growth cycle, all you have to do is pay attention to one thing: What are you pro-crastinating on most that would have the biggest impact if you moved forward on and got it in play?

This is not hard thinking because it's intensely emotional, and emotions are a super form of intelligence: They give an instant read on a situation. Because of this, you don't have to do a lot of research to find your answer. You simply have to ask yourself, "What am I procrastinating on the most, why am I procrastinating, what do I have to do now to move for-ward, what's the deadline for getting something done, and what's the measurable result when it gets done?"

The result you articulate doesn't have to be huge, but it has to be definable and specific.

Three is more than enough.

You'll always have new procrastinations because you're always visualizing bigger and better improvements for your future. But concentrating on and transforming your three biggest procrastinations every day is all you have to do to continually improve in the most satisfying and rewarding fashion.

If you focus on just three every day, in a week you'll have done 21, in a month you'll have done 90, and in a year you'll have done over 1,000. That's likely more progress than you've ever made during any day, any week, any month, or any year in your life.

Additionally, as you become successful at moving through your procrastinations, your goals will constantly increase in size and importance so they remain intellectually stimulating to you. Knocking off something tomorrow that you've already done and isn't really difficult will not be very stimulating. You keep upping the game as you go, naturally leading yourself to higher and higher levels of capability and confidence, and along with that, higher levels of results and achievement.

Nothing external matters more.

An enormous amount of angst in life comes from the belief that, right now, no matter what you're doing, there's something more important you should be doing.

People constantly search outside of themselves for the thing they need to make them better than they are, and are anxious about the idea that the secret to their future suc-cess is controlled by other people and external factors.

You now know that this anxiety-causing notion is not true. The secret is no longer a secret: Your entire future success is a by-product of your daily transformation of your most important procrastinations.

Who you are and who you're becoming will be more contin-ually realized and experienced in the process of transform-ing your procrastinations than in any other activity you could possibly be doing.

You'll also stop relying on other people to satisfy your needs and will let them get on with their lives too.

Feeling bigger every day.

When you identify three procrastinations every evening, transform them in your mind so you're ready to take action the next morning, and then structure the following day so you'll make the progress you envisioned, that next day will automatically feel more expansive. You'll feel greater capa-bility and a higher level of confidence, which will let you take on something even more challenging along the way.

You've likely daydreamed and fantasized about having a personal superpower that continually integrates your whole life, always makes everything simple, and always motivates you to use each day to grow in the best possible way. I hope you now see that you've always had the building blocks for creating this superpower, and that's by making your three most important procrastinations your biggest daily priority.

FOCUS ON THREE EACH DAY

DAILY ACTIVITY

"*WHAT* AM I PROCRASTINATING ABOUT?"

"*WHY* AM I PROCRASTINATING?"

"*HOW* DO I MOVE FORWARD?"

"*WHEN* IS THE DEADLINE?"

"*WHAT* IS THE MEASURABLE RESULT?"

YOUR SUPERPOWER

Conclusion
Your Procrastination Advantage Begins

You now see that almost all the negativity you've experienced in your life associated with procrastination can be transformed into your greatest advantage for creating a high-energy, guilt-free, exciting future.

When I was explaining the Procrastination Priority concept in a workshop, one of my clients told me that it seems like a great exercise but that he personally never procrastinates.

I replied, "Okay. But how about any of your team members? Do they procrastinate?" He said yes, and that it drives him crazy.

I asked him, "Have you done anything about it yet?" He said no, and slowly, a smile grew on his face as he realized there was indeed something he had been procrastinating on.

Ending Stage 1, starting Stage 2.

Yes, we all do it. But how we view procrastination makes all the difference. Far from being a sign of weakness and failure in your past, procrastination is actually a source of unlimited breakthroughs in creative thinking, communication, action, and results over the course of your life.

All the negative experiences you had related to procrastination before you read this book represent Stage 1. Now, you can completely transform these experiences in your mind and see them as having been the necessary preparation for Stage 2. This stage involves realizing that all future experiences of procrastination are simply a way of alerting you to what your most important priorities are for creating your next stage of progress.

You know that you'll procrastinate in the future because you're going to be faced with challenges that are beyond your current capabilities. You'll have to pause in your goal in order to get your mind around the challenge, and you'll have to commit to jumping to a higher level of understanding before moving ahead. You'll know which goals are the most important to pursue because they'll be your biggest procrastinations.

You now have a name for this process: You're just doing your Procrastination Priority. This is a new start, and you have the potential to make radical improvements by shifting to this perspective.

No longer stuck, always moving ahead.

Because procrastination is just a normal, natural, and healthy momentary response to your bigger challenges and opportunities, you no longer have to spend any time and energy on being stuck. Instead, you can use each procrastination as a way of jumping to your next higher achievement.

In this way, procrastination transforms from a factor in your life that stopped you from moving forward into a crucial step in moving ahead with the most important things. Procrastination isn't just something that happens; it's something that *must* happen. It's part of getting to a higher level.

Only three priorities for tomorrow.

Certain things are more important than others. The experience of procrastination automatically tells you which of the things you're putting off are the most important to focus on. Simply ask yourself, "Which are the ones I feel the most pressure, the most anxiety about?" Whatever comes out on top are your priorities right now.

It's unrealistic to think you can complete a list of all your procrastinations in one day. Once you go beyond three big goals in a day, you're entering dangerous territory where you risk your confidence being undermined.

Instead, by focusing on just the three situations that are your best priorities for making breakthroughs, you set yourself up to always have 100 percent achievement days. It's playing the long game, and you'll always feel a sense of success, satisfaction, and forward movement rather than failure and wasted time and energy.

Daily courage a normal activity.

Setting big goals and transforming the obstacles to achieving them requires courage. For most people, one of the problems with courage is that they think it should be an abnormal experience. They think courage should be present only in certain situations—which are ones they probably want to avoid in the first place.

But consider this: What kind of life would you be living if every day required some amount of courage to make a jump, and that jump would show up the following day? Wouldn't this be preferable to a life of courage-avoidance that prevented you from making breakthroughs?

By following through on big goals, making the ones you're procrastinating on the most your priority, you're allowing something that for most people is an exceptional experience to become a normal experience. Every time you allow yourself to go through courage, it produces an extraordinary result.

Because you're using what I call The 4 C's Formula—a process that involves going through the four stages of commitment, courage, capability, and confidence—as a way of making regular progress in transforming your three most important procrastinations every day, courage will become a normal part of your progress for the rest of your life.

And because you're using the Procrastination Priority to determine what you should be focusing on, you'll be using your courage only on the most important things.

Energizing confidence a daily reward.

By adopting the Procrastination Priority mindset and process, you'll identify all the things you're procrastinating on, and your brain will automatically prioritize the top three, which you'll complete the next day. At the end of each day, you'll know the three most important things to do on the following day.

This will be a huge source of energy and confidence, and you'll operate at the optimum level for a thinking, feeling human being with an ambitious future.

Rather than dreading periods of procrastination and feeling guilty about perceived wasted time, you'll look forward with increasing anticipation to a future where each day's trans-formation of your three most important procrastinations pro-duces the following day's jump in your permanent sense of energizing confidence and optimism.

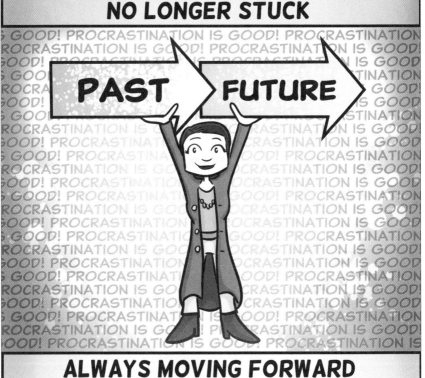

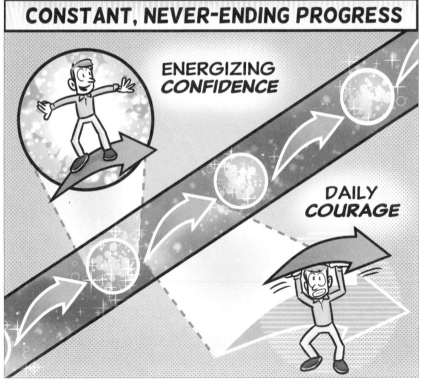

The Strategic Coach Program
Expanding Entrepreneurial Freedom

The Strategic Coach Program, launched in 1989, has qualifications, measurements, structures, and processes that attract a particular type of talented, successful, and ambitious entrepreneur.

One differentiating quality of these Strategic Coach participants is that they recognize that the technology-empowered 21st century is a unique time to be an entrepreneur. It's the first time that a growing number of individuals with no special birth privileges and no special education can achieve almost anything they set their minds to.

These self-motivated individuals who participate in the three levels of Strategic Coach accept that if they can focus on mastering the right mindsets, they can experience increasing breakthroughs for themselves, both personally and professionally, that are new in history.

Procrastination Priority is one of these breakthrough mindsets, and there are dozens more for you to master.

Mindsets that enable entrepreneurs to escape.
Many entrepreneurs have the potential and the willingness to achieve exponential goals in the 21st century, but they are blocked from taking action and making progress because they feel trapped in three ways:

• **Trapped thinking:** They are isolated by their own disconnected creativity, which continually churns out ideas that don't translate into achievement. *At Strategic Coach, entrepreneurs increasingly liberate their thinking to create entirely new practical breakthroughs for themselves and others.*

• **Trapped circumstances:** They are surrounded by people who don't support their ambitions, who actively oppose them, or who try to make them feel guilty about their achievements and dreams. *At Strategic Coach, entrepreneurs learn how to increasingly surround themselves with like-minded and like-motivated individuals in every area of their personal and business lives.*

• **Trapped energy:** They're using much of their daily energy to simply sustain themselves without ever actually experiencing exponential performance and results. They wanted to create a growing business but it turns out that they've only created a job—one that always stays the same. *At Strategic Coach, entrepreneurs continually transform every part of their business organizations so that they become self-managing, and then self-multiplying.*

Mindsets that enable entrepreneurs to achieve.

Around the world, the vast majority of entrepreneurs never get out of these trapped circumstances, but at Strategic Coach, our participants not only escape from these limitations, they also jump to extraordinary levels of achievement, success, and satisfaction.

They never stop growing. Strategic Coach participants continually transform how they think, how they make decisions, how they communicate, and how they take action based on their mastery of dozens of unique entrepreneurial mindsets that have been developed in the Program. These are purely entrepreneurial mindsets, like Procrastination Priority.

We've taken a look at what goes on in the minds of the best

entrepreneurs and have created a thinking system that is custom-designed for them and adjusts to the ambition of each individual.

The Strategic Coach Program provides an accelerating lifetime structure, process, and community for these entrepreneurs to create exponential breakthroughs.

Mindsets that enable entrepreneurs to multiply.

Depending on where you are right now in your life and business, we have a complete set of entrepreneurial mindsets that will immediately jump you up to the next level in terms of your ambition, achievements, and progress. Over the course of your entrepreneurial lifetime, you can move upward through our three levels of mindset measurement and scoring:

1. The Strategic Coach Signature Program: From isolation to teamwork. At this first breakthrough level, you create a Unique Ability Team that allows you to have a Self-Managing Company. Every successful entrepreneur dreams about having this kind of teamwork and this kind of organization. Through the Signature level of the Program, these dreams become a reality. In Strategic Coach, the Self-Managing Company is a practical growth system, not a motivational slogan.

2. The 10x Ambition Program: From teamwork to exponential. You make breakthroughs that transform your life, and your organization becomes a Self-Multiplying Company. Talented entrepreneurs want to free their biggest growth plans from non-supportive relationships, situations, and circumstances. Through the 10x Ambition level of Strategic Coach, their biggest aspirations attract multiplier capabilities, resources, and opportunities.

3. The Game Changer Program: From exponential to transformative. As your entrepreneurial life becomes exponential, your Self-Multiplying Company become trans-formative. *The key evidence of this is that your biggest com-petitors want to become your best students, customers, and promoters.* Game Changer entrepreneurs in Strategic Coach become the leading innovators and cutting-edge teachers in their industries and continually introduce new strategies, methods, and systems that create *new* industries.

Measure yourself, score yourself, get started.

The back cover of this book folds out into a Procrastination Priority Scorecard you can use to score yourself according to the eight mindsets discussed in this book. You can also access a digital copy at *strategiccoach.com/go/ procrastination*. Read through the four statements for each mindset and give yourself a score of 1 to 12 based on where your own mindset falls on the spectrum. Put each mindset's score in the first column at the right, and then add up all eight and put the total at the bottom. Now, think about what scores would represent progress over the next quarter. Write these in the second scoring column, add them up, and write in the total.

When you compare the two scores, you can see where you want to go in terms of your achievements and ambitions. If this fast exercise tells you that you want to multiply in all these areas, contact us today to get started:

The Strategic Coach Program is ready for you! Visit us online at *strategiccoach.com* or call us at 416.531.7399 or 1.800.387.3206.

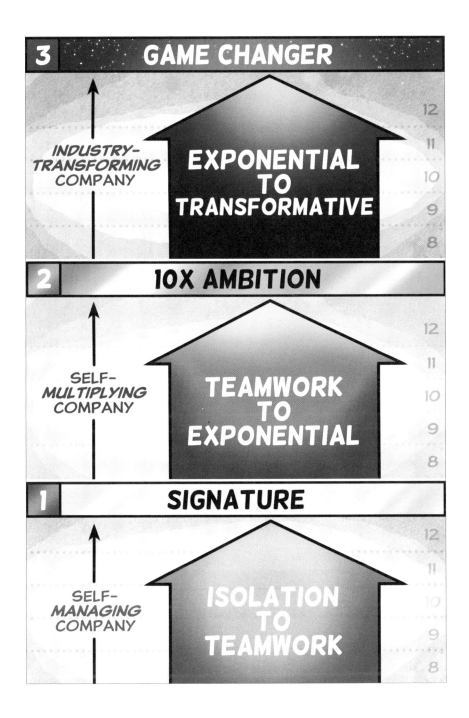

About The Author
Dan Sullivan

Dan Sullivan is the founder and president of The Strategic Coach Inc. and creator of The Strategic Coach® Program, which helps accomplished entrepreneurs reach new heights of success and happiness. He has over 40 years of experience as a strategic planner and coach to entrepreneurial individuals and groups. He is author of over 30 publications, including *The 80% Approach*™, *The Dan Sullivan Question*, *Ambition Scorecard*, *Wanting What You Want*, *The 4 C's Formula*, *The 25-Year Framework*, *The Game Changer*, *The 10x Mind Expander*, *The Mindset Scorecard,* and *The Self-Managing Company*, and is co-author with Catherine Nomura of *The Laws of Lifetime Growth*.